1001
Riddles
For Kids!

JB Publishing Ltd 2017

All rights reserved. No part of this publication may be reproduced, distributed, or transmitted in any form by any means, including photocopying, recording, or other electronic or mechanical methods, without the prior written permission of the publisher, except in the case of brief quotations embodied in critical reviews and certain other commercial uses permitted by copyright law.

1001 Riddles for Kids

Q: What has a face and two hands but no arms or legs?
A: A clock.

Q: A man was driving a black truck. His lights were not on. The moon was not out. A lady was crossing the street. How did the man see her?
A: It was a bright, sunny day.

Q: Can you spell eighty in two letters?
A: A-T.

Q: Every morning the farmer had eggs for breakfast. He owned no chickens and he never got eggs from anyone else's chickens. Where did he get the eggs?
A: From his ducks.

Q: What is the easiest way to double your money?
A: Put it in front of the mirror of course.

Q: If a fifty cent piece and a quarter were on the Empire State Building, which would jump off first?
A: The quarter, because it has less sense (cents).

Q: How does a broom act?
A: With sweeping gestures.

Q: If April showers bring May flowers, what do the Mayflowers bring?
A: Pilgrims.

Q: What has a thumb and four fingers but is not alive?
A: A glove.

Q: If a boy is spanked by his mother and his father, who hurts the most?
A: The boy.

Q: Did you hear the story about the skunk?
A: Never mind, it stinks.

Q: If an egg came floating down the Mississippi River, where did it come from?
A: From a chicken.

Q: What has to be broken before you can use it?
A: An egg.

Q: How many animals did Moses take on the ark?
A: Moses didn't take anything on the ark. Noah did!

Q: How does a fireplace feel?
A: Grate! (Great!)

Q: How should you treat a baby goat?
A: Like a kid.

Q: What has a neck but no head?
A: A bottle.

Q: How does a boat show affection?
A: It hugs the shore.

Q: On what nuts can pictures hang?
A: Walnuts.

Q: How much dirt is there in a hole exactly one foot deep and one foot across?
A: None. A hole is empty.

Q: What gets wetter as it dries?
A: A towel.

Q: Can you read the following? Yy u r yy u b I c u r yy 4 me.
A: Too wise you are, too wise you be, I see you are too wise for me.

Q: What did one broom say to the other broom?
A: "Have you heard the latest dirt?"

Q: How many worms make a foot?
A: Twelve inchworms.

Q: What goes up and doesn't come back down?
A: Your age.

Q: How do pigs write?
A: With a pigpen.

Q: What are southern fathers called?
A: Southpaws.

Q: How many sides does a box have?
A: Two, the inside and the outside.

Q: What belongs to you but is used more by others?
A: Your name.

Q: How did the man feel when he got a big bill from the electric company?
A: He was shocked.

Q: What birds are always unhappy?
A: Bluebirds.

Q: From what number can you take half and leave nothing?
A: The number is 8. Take away the top half and o is left.

Q: Everyone has it and no one can lose it, what is it?
A: A shadow.

Q: How can you tell twin witches apart?
A: It's not easy to tell which witch is which.

Q: What can you hold without touching it?
A: A conversation.

Q: How many feet are in a yard?
A: It depends on how many people are standing in it.

Q: It's been around for millions of years, but it's no more than a month old. What is it?
A: The moon.

Q: How can you tell the difference between a can of chicken soup and a can of tomato soup?
A: Read the label.

Q: What cat lives in the ocean?
A: An octopus.

Q: How many beans can you put in an empty bag?

A: One. After that the bag isn't empty.

Q: What gets wetter the more it dries?
A: towel.

Q: Do you say, "Nine and five is thirteen," or "Nine and five are thirteen"?
A: Neither. Nine and five are fourteen.

Q: What did Napoleon become after his 39th year?
A: 40 years old.

Q: How many acorns grow on the average pine tree?
A: None. Pine trees don't have acorns.

Q: When you look for something, why is it always in the last place you look?
A: Because when you find it, you stop looking.

Q: If a man were born in Greece, raised in Spain, came to America, and died in San Francisco, what is he?
A: Dead.

Q: How does a baby ghost cry?
A: "Boo-hoo! Boo-hoo!"

Q: How is a pig like a horse?
A: When a pig is hungry he eats like a horse, and when a horse is hungry he eats like a pig.

Q: A cowboy rode into town on Friday. He stayed in town for three days and rode out on Friday. How was that possible?
A: Friday was the name of his horse.

Q: What asks no question but demands an answer?
A: A doorbell or a ringing telephone.

Q: What horses keep late hours?
A: Nightmares.

Q: How is a burning candle like thirst?
A: A bit of water ends both of them.

Q: One night, a king and a queen went into a castle. There was nobody in the castle, and no one came out of the castle. In the morning, three people came out of the castle. Who were they?
A: The knight (night), the king, and the queen.

Q: What animal makes the most of its food?
A: The giraffe. It makes a little go a long way.

Q: What insect can be spelled with just one letter?
A: Bee.

Q: How do you make notes of stone?
A: Rearrange the letters.

Q: Railroad crossing, watch out of cars. Can you spell that without any "r's"?
A: T-H-A-T.

Q: What animal doesn't believe anything?
A: Sheep. They always say, "Bah! Bah!"

Q: What is a bee with a low buzz?
A: A mumble bee.

Q: How do you make a cigarette lighter?
A: Take out the tobacco.

Q: What has a face and two hands, but no arms or legs?
A: A clock.

Q: What always comes into a house through the keyhole?
A: A key.

Q: What did Tennessee?
A: He saw what Arkansas.

Q: How are 2 plus 2 equal 5 and your left hand alike?
A: Neither is right.

Q: What has to be broken before you can use it?
A: An egg.

Q: Spell "pound" in two letters.
A: Lb.

Q: How can you double your money?
A: Look at it in a mirror.

Q: How do we know that mountain goats have feet?
A: Because they are sure-footed.

Q: Lives in winter, dies in summer, and grows with its roots upward. What is it?
A: An icicle.

Q: On what kind of ships do students study?
A: Scholarships.

Q: How can you make seven even?
A: Take away the letter S.

Q: How do we know Rome was built at night?
A: Because Rome wasn't built in day.

Q: It starts out tall, but the longer it stands, the shorter it grows. What is it?
A: A candle.

Q: If you want to get rich, why should you keep your mouth shut?
A: Because silence is golden.

Q: How can you name the capital of every U.S. state in two seconds?
A: Washington, D.C.

Q: How can you place a pencil on the floor so that no one can jump over it?
A: Put it next to the wall.

Q: What belongs to you but is used more by others?
A: Your name.

Q: If cows talked all at once, what would they say?
A: Nothing. Cows can't talk.

Q: How do you make a lemon drop?
A: Hold it and then let go.

Q: How can you make a fire with only one stick?
A: Easy. Just make sure it's a matchstick.

Q: What goes up and never comes down?
A: Your age.

Q: If six children and two dogs were under an umbrella, how come none of them got wet?
A: Because it wasn't raining.

Q: How do you file a nail?
A: Under the letter N.

Q: How can you be sure you have counterfeit money?
A: If it's a three-dollar bill, you can be sure.

Q: How can a man go 8 days without sleep?
A: He only sleeps at night.

Q: What belongs to you, but is used more by others?
A: Your name.

Q: What have eyes but can't see?
A: Needles, storms and potatoes.

Q: How can you go without sleep for seven days and not be tired?
A: Sleep at night.

Q: I'm full of keys but I can't open any door. What am I?
A: A piano.

Q: What did the big watch hand say to the little watch hand?
A: "Don't go away, I'll be back in an hour."

Q: What did the big watch hand say to the small hand?
A: "Got a minute?"

Q: How can you drop an egg 3 feet without breaking it?
A: Drop it 4 feet. For the first 3 feet the egg will not hit anything.

Q: What has a thumb and four fingers but is not alive?
A: A glove.

Q: What did the big chimney say to the little chimney?
A: "You are too young to smoke."

Q: What do you get if you cross a cat with a laughing hyena?
A: A giggle puss.

Q: What has two legs like an Indian, two eyes like an Indian, two hands like an Indian, looks just like an Indian-but is not an Indian?
A: The picture of an Indian.

Q: A man found an old coin and declared that the date on it was 150 B.C. This could not be true. Why?
A: Because B.C. is counting backwards from the birth of Christ. If Christ hadn't been born yet, there were no dates in B.C. yet.

Q: What did the bee say to the flower?
A: "Hello, honey!"

Q: What do you get if you feed a lemon to your cat?
A: A sourpuss.

Q: What is the center of gravity?
A: The letter. Y.

Q: Which is heavier, a pound of bricks or a pound of feathers?
A: The same – a pound is a pound.

Q: What did one wall say to the other?
A: "I'll meet you at the corner."

Q: What fish is a bargain?
A: A sailfish (sale fish).

Q: What is shaped like a box, has no feet and runs up and down?
A: An elevator.

Q: I'm light as a feather, yet the strongest man can't hold me for more than 5 minutes. What am I?
A: Breath.

Q: What did one car muffler say to the other car muffler?
A: "Am I exhausted!"

Q: What fly has laryngitis?
A: A horsefly (hoarse fly).

Q: What is pointed in one direction and headed in the other?
A: A pin.

Q: Can you name three consecutive days without using the words Wednesday, Friday, and Sunday?
A: Yesterday, today, and tomorrow.

Q: What did one candle say to the other candle?
A: "Going out tonight?"

Q: What food are you able to can?
A: Cannibal (can able) food.

Q: What is ploughed but never planted?
A: Snow.

Q: Timmy's mother had three children. The first was named April, the next was named May. What was the name of the third child?
A: Timmy of course.

Q: What did one arithmetic book say to the other arithmetic book?
A: "Boy, do I have problems!"

Q: What food is good for the brain?
A: Noodle soup.

Q: What is on your arm and in the sea?
A: A muscle (mussel).

Q: What kind of coat can only be put on when wet?
A: A coat of paint.

Q: What colour was Napoleon's white horse?
A: White.

Q: What gets around everywhere?

A: Belts.

Q: What increases its value by being turned upside down?
A: The number 6.

Q: What occurs once in a minute, twice in a moment, and never in one thousand years?
A: The letter M.

Q: What cap is never removed?
A: Your kneecap.

Q: What gives milk and has one horn?
A: A milk truck.

Q: What is never out of sight?
A: The letter S.

Q: What has three feet but cannot walk?
A: A yardstick.

Q: What can run but can't walk?
A: Water.

Q: What has fifty heads and fifty tails?
A: Fifty pennies.

Q: What is locomotion?
A: A crazy dance.

Q: What runs, but never walks, often murmurs – never talks, has a bed but never sleeps, has a mouth but never eats?
A: A river.

Q: What can you break without touching it?
A: Your promise.

Q: What goes around in circles and makes kids happy?
A: A merry-go-round.

Q: What is in the middle of March?
A: The letter R.

Q: If you are running in a race and you pass the person in second place, what place are you in?
A: Second place.

Q: What did the boy squirrel say to the girl squirrel?
A: "I'm nuts about you."

Q: What do you call a greasy chicken?
A: A slick chick.

Q: What is dark but made by light?
A: A shadow.

Q: What gets sharper the more you use it?
A: Your brain.

Q: What does a caterpillar do on New Year's Day?
A: Turns over a new leaf.

Q: What is the difference between a tickle and a wise guy?
A: One is fun, the other thinks he's fun.

Q: What is an Eskimo father?

A: A cold pop.

Q: If I have it, I don't share it. If I share it, I don't have it. What is it?
A: A secret.

Q: What do you get if you cross an insect and a rabbit?
A: Bugs Bunny.

Q: What is the left side of an apple?
A: The part that you don't eat.

Q: What invention allows you to see through walls?
A: A window.

Q: What can you catch but not throw?
A: A cold.

Q: What do people make that you can't see?
A: Noise.

Q: What is the most valuable fish?
A: Goldfish.

Q: What is always behind the times?
A: The back of a clock.

Q: How many months have 28 days?
A: All 12 months.

Q: What did the tree say to the woodpecker?
A: "You bore me."

Q: What is the opposite of restaurant?

A: Workerant.

Q: What is a small cad?
A: A caddy.

Q: They come out at night without being called, and are lost in the day without being stolen. What are they?
A: Stars.

Q: What did the man say when he got a big phone bill?
A: "Who said talk is cheap?"

Q: What is the science of shopping?
A: Biology (buy-ology).

Q: What is a dark horse?
A: A nightmare.

Q: What is full of holes but can still hold water?
A: A sponge.

Q: What did the man do when he got a big gas bill?
A: He exploded.

Q: What is a broken down hot rod?
A: A shot rod.

Q: What did Columbus see on his right hand when he discovered America?
A: Five fingers.

Q: Two in front, two in behind, and one in the middle. How many are there?

A: Three.

Q: What did the father tree say to his son?
A: "You're a chip off the old block."

Q: What do you draw without a pencil or paper?
A: A window shade.

Q: What has four fingers and thumb but is not a hand?
A: A glove.

Q: I'm tall when I'm young and I'm short when I'm old. What am I?
A: A candle.

Q: What did the light switch say to the girl?
A: "You turn me on. "

Q: What did the chicks say to the miser?
A: "Cheap! Cheap!"

Q: What has a neck but no head?
A: A bottle.

Q: In a one-story pink house, there was a pink person, a pink cat, a pink fish, a pink computer, a pink chair, a pink table, a pink telephone, a pink shower– everything was pink. What color were the stairs?
A: There weren't any stairs, it was a one storey house.

Q: What did the girl squirrel answer back?
A: "You're nuts so bad yourself."

Q: What did the electric plug say to the wall?

A: "Socket to me!"

Q: What has a hundred limbs but can't walk?
A: A tree.

Q: What has hands but can not clap?
A: A clock.

Q: What did the fly say to the flypaper?
A: "I'm stuck on you."

Q: What did the girl watch say to the boy watch?
A: "Keep your hands to yourself".

Q: What has a foot on each side and one in the middle?
A: A yardstick.

Q: A house has 4 walls. All of the walls are facing south, and a bear is circling the house. What color is the bear?
A: The house is on the north pole, so the bear is white.

Q: What does an envelope say when you lick it?
A: Nothing. It just shuts up.

Q: What is ice?
A: Skid stuff.

Q: What happens if you talk when there is food in your mouth?
A: You will have said a mouthful.

Q: What is at the end of a rainbow?
A: The letter W.

Q: What kind of bath can you take without water?
A: A sun bath.

Q: What kind of meat doesn't stand up?
A: Lean meat.

Q: What goes through water but doesn't get wet?
A: A ray of light.

Q: What starts with the letter "t", is filled with "t" and ends in "t"?
A: A teapot.

Q: What kind of apple has a short temper?
A: A crab apple.

Q: What kind of money do monsters use?
A: Weirdo (weird dough).

Q: What do elephants have that no other animals have?
A: Baby elephants.

Q: A girl is sitting in a house at night that has no lights on at all. There is no lamp, no candle, nothing. Yet she is reading. How?
A: The woman is blind and is reading braille.

Q: What is the first thing you see when you understand something?
A: You see the light.

Q: What kind of paper can you tear?
A: Terrible (tearable) paper.

Q: What goes through a door but never goes in or out?
A: A keyhole.

Q: You walk into a room with a match, a karosene lamp, a candle, and a fireplace. Which do you light first?
A: The match.

Q: What is the first thing you put into a room?
A: Your feet.

Q: What kind of apple isn't an apple?
A pineapple.

Q: What goes out black and comes in white?
A: A black cow in a snowstorm.

Q: What gets wetter and wetter the more it dries?
A: A Towel.

Q: What is the first thing you do in the morning?
A: You wake up.

Q: What kind of water can't freeze?
A: Hot water.

Q: What goes further the slower it goes?
A: Money.

Q: You draw a line. Without touching it, how do you make the line longer?
A: You draw a shorter line next to it, and it becomes the longer line.

Q: What is the difference between here and there?
A: The letter T.

Q: What knights rode camels?
A: The Arabian Nights (knights).

Q: What goes from side to side, and up and down, but never moves?
A: A road.

Q: Which weighs more, a pound of feathers or a pound of bricks?
A: Neither, they both weigh one pound.

Q: What is the difference between a pear and a pearl?
A: The letter L.

Q: What letter is like a vegetable?
A: The letter P.

Q: What do they do with a tree after they chop it down?
A: Chop it up.

Q: How many months have 28 days?
A: All 12 months.

Q: What is the best day to go to the beach?
A: Sunday.

Q: What pet is always found on the floor?
A: A carpet.

Q: What does grass say when it is cut?

A: "I don't mow (know)."

Q: Name four days of the week that start with the letter "t"?
A: Tuesday, Thursday, today, and tomorrow.

Q: What is drawn by everyone without pen or pencil?
A: Breath.

Q: What sea creature can add?
A: An octoplus.

Q: What do you lose every time you stand up?
A: Your lap.

Q: A train leaves from Halifax, Nova Scotia heading towards Vancouver, British Columbia at 120 km/h. Three hours later, a train leaves Vancouver heading towards Halifax at 180 km/h. Assume there's exactly 6000 kilometers between Vancouver and Halifax. When they meet, which train is closer to Halifax?
A: Both trains would be at the same spot when they meet therefore they are both equally close to Halifax.

Q: What is a zebra?
A: A horse with venetian blinds.

Q: What state has a friendly greeting for everyone?
A: Ohio.

Q: If you take half from a half dollar, what do you have?
A: A dollar.

Q: What goes around and around the wood but never goes into the wood?
A: The bark on a tree.

Q: What does Brazil produce that no other country produces?
A: Brazilians.

Q: What is Dracula's favourite sport?
A: Bat-minton (badminton).

Q: What colour is rain?
A: Water colour.

Q: Two mothers and two daughters went out to eat, everyone ate one burger, yet only three burgers were eaten in all. How is this possible?
A: They were a grandmother, mother and daughter.

Q: What is a sound sleeper?
A: Someone who snores.

Q: What stays hot in the refrigerator?
A: Mustard.

Q: What code message is the same from left to right, right to left, upside down and right side up?
A: SOS.

Q: A man was outside taking a walk, when it started to rain. The man didn't have an umbrella and he wasn't wearing a hat. His clothes got soaked, yet not a single hair on his head got wet. How could this happen?
A: The man was bald.

Q: What is a Mexican weather report?
A: Chilli today, hot tamale.

Q: What time is it when a clock strikes thirteen?
A: Time to get it fixed.

Q: What can you put in a glass but never take out of it?
A: A crack.

Q: A cowboy rides into town on Friday, stays for three days, then leaves on Friday. How did he do it?
A: His horse's name was Friday.

Q: What is a calf after it is six months old?
A: Seven months old.

Q: What kind of animal tells little white lies?
A: An amphibian.

Q: What can you hold in your left hand but not in your right hand?
A: Your right elbow.

Q: You walk across a bridge and you see a boat full of people yet there isn't a single person on board. How is that possible?
A: All the people on the boat are married.

Q: What insect runs away from everything?
A: A flea (flee).

Q: What is a good way to get fat?
A: Fry up some bacon.

Q: What can you add to a bucket of water that will make it weigh less?
A: Holes.

Q: A boy was rushed to the hospital emergency room. The ER doctor saw the boy and said, "I cannot operate on this boy. He is my son." But the doctor was not the boy's father. How could that be?
A: The doctor was his mom.

Q: What insect gets A's in English?
A: A spelling bee.

Q: What is a parrot?
A: A wordy birdy.

Q: What can turn without moving?
A: Milk. It can turn sour.

Q: What can run but can't walk?
A: A drop of water.

Q: What has two hands but no arms?
A: A clock.

Q: What is a sleeping bag?
A: A knapsack (nap sack).

Q: Is it better to say, "The yolk of an egg is white," or "The yolk of an egg are white?"
A: Neither. An egg yolk is yellow.

Q: How far can a dog run into the woods?

A: The dog can run into the woods only to the half of the wood – than it would run out of the woods.

Q: What has teeth but no mouth?
A: A comb or a saw.

Q: What is a sleeping bull?
A: A bull dozer.

Q: What can a whole apple do that half an apple can't do?
A: It can look round.

Q: If there are 3 apples and you take away 2, how many do you have?
A: If you take 2 apples, then you have of course 2.

Q: What has four legs and a back but no body?
A: A chair.

Q: What is a vampire's favourite soup?
A: Alpha-bat (alphabet) soup.

Q: What baby is born with whiskers?
A: A kitten.

Q: Beth's mother has three daughters. One is called Lara, the other one is Sara. What is the name of the third daughter?
A: Beth.

Q: What happens when you throw a green rock in the Red Sea?
A: It gets wet.

Q: What is a very hard subject?
A: The study of rocks.

Q: What animals follow everywhere you go?
A: Your calves.

Q: You have a 5 gallon bucket and a 3 gallon bucket with as much water as you need, but no other measuring devices. Fill the 5 gallon bucket with exactly 4 gallons of water.
A: Fill the 5 gallon bucket all the way up. Pour it into the 3 gallon bucket until it is full. Empty the 3 gallon bucket. Pour the remaining 2 gallons into the 3 gallon bucket. Fill the 5 gallon bucket all the way up. Finish filling the 3 gallon bucket.

Q: What doesn't get any wetter no matter how much it rains?
A: The ocean.

Q: What is a ghost's favourite rock?
A: Tombstone.

Q: What "bus" crossed the ocean?
A: Columbus.

Q: What's full of holes but still holds water?
A: A sponge.

Q: What goes up and down but doesn't move?
A: A staircase.

Q: What is a wet cat?
A: A drizzle puss.

Q: Two men dig a hole in five days. How many days would it take them to dig half a hole?
A: None. You can't dig half a hole.

Q: If an electric train is going east at 60 miles an hour and there is a strong westerly wind, which way does the smoke from the train drift?
A: There is no smoke coming from electric trains.

Q: What goes around a yard but doesn't move?
A: A fence.

Q: What is another name for a telephone booth?
A: A chatterbox.

Q: Is it better to write on a full or on an empty stomach?
A: Neither. Paper is much better.

Q: Say Racecar backwards.
A: 'Racecar backwards'.

Q: What flower does everyone have?
A: Tulips (two lips).

Q: What is bought by the yard and worn by the foot?
A: A carpet.

Q: On which side does a chicken have the most feathers?
A: On the outside.

Q: What do the numbers 11, 69, and 88 all have in common?
A: The read the same right side up and upside down.

Q: What kind of bulbs don't need water?
A: Light bulbs.

Q: What kind of lock is on a hippie's door?
A: A padlock.

Q: How can you throw a ball as hard as you can, to only have it come back to you, even if it doesn't bounce off anything?
A: Throw the ball straight up in the air.

Q: What ten letter word starts with g-a-s?
A: Automobile.

Q: Why are diapers like $10 bills?
A: Because you have to change them.

Q: My name is Ruger, I live on a farm. There are four other dogs on the farm with me. Their names are Snowy, Flash, Speedy and Brownie. What do you think the fifth dog's name is?
A: Ruger.

Q: What song does a car radio play?
A: A cartoon (car, tune).

Q: Why are most cows noisy?
A: Because they have horns.

Q: I am an odd number. Take away one letter and I become even. What number am I?
A: Seven (take away the 's' and it becomes 'even').

Q: What piece of wood is like a king?

A: A ruler.

Q: Why are pants always too short?
A: Two feet are always sticking out.

Q: What word looks the same backwards and upside down?
A: SWIMS.

Q: What person is always in a hurry?
A: A Russian.

Q: Why are rivers lazy?
A: Because they never get off their beds.

Q: A boy fell off a 30-meter ladder but did not get hurt. Why not?
A: He fell off the bottom step.

Q: What people travel the most?
A: Romans.

Q: What would you call a beautiful cat?
A: A glamour puss.

Q: Using only addition, how do you add eight 8's and get the number 1000?
A: 888 + 88 + 8 + 8 + 8 = 1000.

Q: What people are like the end of a book?
A: The Finnish.

Q: Why did Batman go to the pet shop?
A: To buy a Robin.

Q: How do dog catchers get paid?
A: By the pound.

Q: What paper makes you itch?
A: Scratch paper.

Q: Why did the cowboy ride his horse?
A: Because the horse was too heavy to carry.

Q: What never asks questions but is often answered?
A: A doorbell.

Q: What kind of watch is best for people who don't like time on their hands?
A: A pocket watch.

Q: Why did the kid keep his shirt on when he took a bath?
A: Because the label said "Wash and Wear."

Q: What belongs to you but other people use it more than you?
A: Your name.

Q: What kind of tree do you find in the kitchen?
A: A pantry.

Q: Why did the man put a clock under his desk?
A: He wanted to work overtime.

Q: I have a large money box, 48 centemeters square and 42 centemeters tall. Roughly how many coins can I place in my empty money box?
A: Just one, after which it will no longer be empty.

Q: What kind of table has no legs?
A: A multiplication table.

Q: Why did the ocean roar?
A: Because it had crabs in its bed.

Q: What does this mean? I RIGHT I
A: Right between the eyes.

Q: What kind of coach has no wheels?
A: A football **coach**.

Q: What kind of key opens a casket?
A: A skeleton key.

Q: What 5-letter word becomes shorter when you add two letters to it?
A: Short.

Q: What kind of star wears sunglasses?
A: A movie star.

Q: Why did the window pane blush?
A: It saw the weather-strip.

Q: Imagine you're in a room that is filling with water. There are no windows or doors. How do you get out?
A: Stop imagining.

Q: What kind of hogs do you find on highways?
A: Road hogs.

Q: What wears shoes but has no feet?
A: The sidewalk.

Q: The more you take, the more you leave behind. What are they?
A: Footprints.

Q: What kind of electricity do they have in Washington?
A: D.C. (Direct Current).

Q: What kind of bird is like a letter?
A: A jaybird.

Q: What two keys can't open any door?
A: A monkey and a donkey.

Q: What kind of cup doesn't hold water?
A: A cupcake.

Q: What kind of cattle laugh?
A: Laughingstock.

Q: What invention lets you look right through a wall?
A: A window.

Q: What time is the same spelled backward or forward?
A: Noon.

Q: Who has friends for lunch?
A: A cannibal.

Q: What has a foot but no legs?
A: A snail.

Q: Why did the man have to fix the horn of his car?
A: Because it didn't give a hoot.

Q: Why do you go to bed?
A: Because the bed will not come to you.

Q: Poor people have it. Rich people need it. If you eat it you die. What is it?
A: Nothing.

Q: Why did the kid put his clock in the oven.
A: He wanted to have a hot time.

Q: Why don't bananas ever get lonely?
A: Because they go around in bunches.

Q: What comes down but never goes up?
A: Rain.

Q: Why did the kid avoid the cemetery?
A: He wouldn't be caught dead there.

Q: Why is an old car like a baby playing?
A: Because it goes with a rattle.

Q: I'm tall when I'm young and I'm short when I'm old. What am I?
A: A candle.

Q: Why did Jack and Jill roll down the hill?
A: It beats walking.

Q: Why do people work as bakers?
A: Because they knead (need) the dough.

Q: Mary's father has 5 daughters – Nana, Nene, Nini, Nono. What is the fifth daughters name?

A: If you answered Nunu, you are wrong. It's Mary.

Q: Why can't you read a story about a bed?
A: It hasn't been made up yet.

Q: Why is the moon like a dollar?
A: It has four quarters.

Q: How can a pants pocket be empty and still have something in it?
A: It can have a hole in it.

Q: Why can't a mind reader read your mind?
A: He could-if you had one!

Q: Why isn't a dime worth as much today as it used to be?
A: Because the dimes (times) have changed.

Q: What goes up when rain comes down?
A: An umbrella.

Q: What trees come in two's?
A: Pear (pair) trees.

Q: Which end of a bus is it best to get off?
A: It doesn't matter. Both ends stop.

Q: What is the longest word in the dictionary?
A: Smiles, because there is a mile between each 's'.

Q: Who never gets his hair wet in the shower?
A: A bald man.

Q: Why shouldn't you believe a person in bed?

A: Because he is lying.

Q: If I drink, I die. If i eat, I am fine. What am I?
A: A fire.

Q: Who can marry a lot of wives and still be single?
A: A minister.

Q: Why was the boy's suit rusty?
A: It was guaranteed to wear like iron.

Q: Throw away the outside and cook the inside, then eat the outside and throw away the inside. What is it?
A: Corn on the cob, because you throw away the husk, cook and eat the kernels, and throw away the cob.

Q: Who always goes to bed with shoes on?
A: A horse.

Q: Why was the girl named Sugar?
A: Because she was so refined.

Q: What word becomes shorter when you add two letters to it?
A: Short.

Q: Where do frogs sit?
A: On toadstools.

Q: Why was the horse all charged up?
A: Because it ate haywire.

Q: What travels around the world but stays in one spot?
A: A stamp.

Q: Where did the knights study?
A: In knight (night) school.

Q: Why do mummies tell no secrets?
A: Because they keep things under wraps.

Q: What has 4 eyes but can't see?
A: Mississippi.

Q: Where can you always find money?
A: In the dictionary.

Q: When is a man like a dog?
A: When he is a boxer.

Q: If I have it, I don't share it. If I share it, I don't have it. What is it?
A: A Secret.

Q: When prices are going up, what remains stationary?
A: Writing paper and envelopes.

Q: When is the moon heaviest?
A: When it is full.

Q: Take away my first letter, and I still sound the same. Take away my last letter, I still sound the same. Even take away my letter in the middle, I will still sound the same. I am a five-letter word. What am I?
A: EMPTY

Q: What two things can't you have for breakfast?
A: Lunch and dinner.

Q: When is a chair like a fabric?
A: When it is sat in (satin).

Q: What has hands but can not clap?
A: A clock.

Q: When does a chair dislike you?
A: When it can't bear you.

Q: Where do ants go when they want to eat?
A: To a restaur-ant.

Q: What can you catch but not throw?
A: A cold.

Q: When a dirty kid has finished taking a bath, what is still dirty?
A: The bathtub.

Q: Where do baby trees go to school?
A: To a tree nursery.

Q: A house has 4 walls. All of the walls are facing south, and a bear is circling the house. What color is the bear?
A: The house is on the north pole, so the bear is white.

Q: What word if pronounced right is wrong but if pronounced wrong is right?
A: Wrong.

Q: Where do they put crying children?
A: In a bawl (ball) park.

Q: What is at the end of a rainbow?
A: The letter W.

Q: What weighs more: a pound of lead or a pound of feathers?
A: They weigh the same.

Q: Where was Solomon's temple?
A: On his head.

Q: What is as light as a feather, but even the world's strongest man couldn't hold it for more than a minute?
A: His breath.

Q: Did you hear the story about the oatmeal?
A: Never mind. It's a lot of mush.

Q: A police officer had a brother, but the brother had no brother. How could this be?
A: The police officer was a woman.

Q: Why is Saturday night important to Julius's girl friend?
A: That's when Julius Caesar (sees her).

Q: Why is a garden like a story?
A: They both have plots.

Q: What starts with the letter "t", is filled with "t" and ends in "t"?
A: A teapot.

Q: What amusement park ride breaks up romances?

A: A merry-go-round. When the ride is over, people stop going around with each other.

Q: How can you come face-to-face with a hungry, angry lion, dare him to fight, and still be unafraid?
A: Walk calmly to the next cage.

Q: Why do people feel stronger on Saturdays and Sundays?
A: Because all the other days are week (weak) days.

Q: Why is it so wet in Great Britain?
A: Because of all the kings and queens that reigned (rained) there.

Q: What can you hold without touching it?
A: A conversation.

Q: Phil played the harmonica so well he now plays with what symphony orchestra?
A: The Philharmonica.

Q: For how long a period of time did Cain hate his brother?
A: As long as he was Abel (able).

Q: What is so delicate that saying its name breaks it?
A: Silence.

Q: Why is an inexpensive dog a bad watchdog?
A: Because a bargain (barkin') dog does not bite.

Q: Why is a rabbit's nose always shiny?
A: Because his powder puff is on the wrong end.

Q: You walk into a room with a match, a karosene lamp, a candle, and a fireplace. Which do you light first?
A: The match.

Q: If you scratch a horse's hair on a cat gut, what do you get?
A: Violin music.

Q: Did you hear about the hold-up in the yard?
A: Two clothespins held up a pair of pants.

Q: What can you make that you can't see?
A: Noise.

Q: Why is Ireland so rich?
A: Because its capital is always Dublin (doublin').

Q: Why is the letter "A" like a flower?
A: Because a bee (B) comes after it.

Q: A man was driving his truck. His lights were not on. The moon was not out. Up ahead, a woman was crossing the street. How did he see her?
A: It was a bright and sunny day.

Q: If a band plays music in a thunderstorm, who is most likely to get hit by lightning?
A: The conductor.

Q: A policeman saw a truck driver going the wrong way down a one-way street, but didn't give him a ticket. Why not?
A: The truck driver was walking.

Q: What question must always be answered "Yes"?
A: What does "Y"-"E"-"S" spell?

Q: Why was the little horse unhappy?
A: Because every time it wanted something, its mother would say, "Neigh."

Q: Why should you never tell secrets in a garden?
A: Because the corn has ears, the potatoes have eyes, and the beans talk (beanstalk).

Q: What kind of tree can you carry in your hand?
A: A palm.

Q: How do they dance in Arabia?
A: Sheik-to-sheik (cheek).

Q: Can you spell jealousy with two letters?
A: NV (envy).

Q: What is bought by the yard and worn by the foot?
A: Carpet.

Q: Why is a shirt with 8 buttons so interesting?
A: Because you fascinate (fasten 8).

Q: Why shouldn't you cry if your cow falls off a mountain?
A: There's no use in crying over spilt milk.

Q: If an electric train is travelling south, which way is the smoke going?
A: There is no smoke, it's an electric train.

Q: Did you hear the story about the piece of butter?

A: Never mind. I don't want to spread it around.

Q: How can you avoid falling hair?
A: Get out of the way.

Q: What can you break without touching it?
A: A promise.

Q: Why was the Lone Ranger poor?
A: Because he was always saying, "I owe (heigh-ho) Silver!"

Q: Why was the mother flea so sad?
A: Because her children were going to the dogs.

Q: You draw a line. Without touching it, how do you make the line longer?
A: You draw a shorter line next to it, and it becomes the longer line.

Q: What animals are poor dancers?
A: Four-legged ones, because they have two left feet.

Q: How can you jump off a 50-foot ladder without getting hurt?
A: Jump off the bottom rung.

Q: How can you make seven even?
A: Take away the "S".

Q: Why is a pig's tail like S A.M.?
A: They are both twirly (too early).

Q: Why is it dangerous to walk around the country in the spring?

A: Because then the grass is full of blades, the flowers have pistils (pistols), and the trees are shooting.

Q: What has one eye but cannot see?
A: A needle.

Q: What did the football say to the football player?
A: "I get a kick out of YOU."

Q: What animal breaks the law?
A: A cheetah.

Q: What has teeth but can't eat?
A: A comb.

Q: Why does a lion kneel before it springs?
A: Because it is preying (praying).

Q: Why do the hippies study the stars?
A: Because they are so far out.

Q: Why did the nutty kid throw a bucket of water out of the window?
A: He wanted to make a big splash.

Q: A man leaves home and turns left three times, only to return home facing two men wearing masks. Who are those two men?
A: A Catcher and Umpire.

Q: What did one firecracker say to the other firecracker?
A: "My pop is bigger than your pop."

Q: If you were walking in a jungle and saw a lion, what time would it be?
A: Time to run.

Q: What do you call bears with no ears?
A: "B".

Q: Why do windows squeak when you open them?
A: Because they have panes (pains).

Q: Why does a baby duck walk softly?
A: Because it is a baby and it can't walk, hardly.

Q: Why do firemen wear red suspenders?
A: To keep their pants up.

Q: Which weighs more, a pound of feathers or a pound of bricks?
A: Neither, they both weigh one pound.

Q: What dance do you do when summer is over?
A: Tango (tan go).

Q: If five boys beat up one boy, what time would it be?
A: Five to one.

Q: What word has five letters but sounds like it only has one?
A: Queue.

Q: Why doesn't Sweden export cattle?
A: Because she wants to keep her Stockholm (stock home).

Q: Why don't bananas snore?
A: They don't want to wake up the rest of the bunch.

Q: How many months have 28 days?
A: All 12 months.

Q: What dance do hippies hate?
A: A square dance.

Q: How do you spell a hated opponent with three letters?
A: NME (enemy).

Q: How many animals did Moses take on the ark?
A: None, it was Noah.

Q: Why is a barefoot boy like an Eskimo?
A: The barefoot boy wears no shoes and the Eskimo wears snowshoes.

Q: Why don't flies fly through screen doors?
A: Because they don't want to strain themselves.

Q: A frog jumped into a pot of cream and started treading. He soon felt something solid under his feet and was able to hop out of the pot. What did the frog feel under his feet?
A: The frog felt butter under his feet, because he churned the cream and made butter.

Q: What dance did the Pilgrims do?
A: The Plymouth Rock.

Q: How did the chimpanzee escape from his cage?
A: He used a monkey wrench.

Q: Why do ships use knots instead of miles?
A: To keep the sea tide (tied).

Q: Why is a cat like a penny?
A: Because it has a head on one side and a tail on the other.

Q: A horse is on a 24-foot chain and wants an apple that is 26 feet away. How can the horse get to the apple?
A: The chain is not attached to anything.

Q: What broadcasting company has the best horror shows?
A: The Ghost-to-Ghost network.

Q: How can you tell when a mummy is angry?
A: When he flips his lid.

Q: Why is a mouse like hay?
A: Because the cat'll (cattle) eat it.

Q: Why are spiders like tops?
A: Because they are always spinning.

Q: Why did the nutty kid throw a glass of water out of the window?
A: He wanted to see a waterfall.

Q: If a blue house is made out of blue bricks, a yellow house is made out of yellow bricks and a pink house is made out of pink bricks, what is a green house made of?
A: Glass.

Q: What do birds say on Halloween?
A: "Twick or tweet."

Q: Spell mousetrap with three letters.
A: C-A-T.

Q: When is a well-dressed lion like a weed?
A: When he's a dandelion (dandy lion).

Q: Why do squirrels spend so much time in trees?
A: To get away from all the nuts on the ground.

Q: What goes up a chimney down but can't come down a chimney up?
A: An umbrella.

Q: What holiday does Dracula celebrate in November?
A: Fangsgi ving (Thanksgiving).

Q: What bird always runs from a fight?
A: A canary, because it is yellow.

Q: Where does a vampire take a bath?
A: In the bat-room (bathroom).

Q: What sea creature has to have a good reason for doing anything?
A: A porpoise (purpose).

Q: We see it once in a year, twice in a week, and never in a day. What is it?
A: The letter "E".

Q: What has eight feet and can sing?
A: A barbershop quartet.

Q: What animal has a chip on its shoulder?
A: A chipmunk.

Q: Where does the sandman keep his sleeping sand?
A: In his knapsack (nap sack).

Q: Why did the lady mouse want to move?
A: She was tired of living in a hole in the wall.

Q: Mr. Blue lives in the blue house, Mr. Pink lives in the pink house, and Mr. Brown lives in the brown house. Who lives in the white house?
A: The president.

Q: What happened to the kid who ran away with the circus?
A: The police made him bring it back.

Q: How does an octopus go to war?
A: Armed.

Q: Where were the first French fries made?
A: In Greece (grease).

Q: Why did the nature lover plant bird seed?
A: He wanted to grow canaries.

Q: They come out at night without being called, and are lost in the day without being stolen. What are they?
A: Stars.

Q: What game do you play in water?
A: Swimming pool.

Q: If an African lion fought an African tiger, who would win?
A: Neither. There are no tigers in Africa.

Q: Why are oranges like bells?
A: You can peel (peal) both of them.

Q: Why didn't the man believe what the sardine said?
A: It sounded too fishy.

Q: How do you make the number one disappear?
A: Add the letter G and it's "GONE".

Q: What game do ghost children play?
A: Haunt and seek.

Q: If you cross a lion and a mouse, what will you have?
A: A mighty mouse.

Q: When is it difficult to get your watch off your wrist?
A: When it's ticking (sticking) there.

Q: Why do bees hum?
A: Because they don't know the words.

Q; What goes up but never comes down?
A: Your age.

Q: What fish sings songs?
A: A tuna fish.

Q: If you plug your electric blanket into the toaster, what happens?
A: You pop up all night.

Q: Why did the lady hold her ears when she passed the chickens?
A: Because she didn't want to hear their foul (fowl) language.

Q: Why do cows wear bells?
A: Because their horns don't work.

Q: Tuesday, Sam and Peter went to a restaurant to eat lunch. After eating lunch, they paid the bill. But Sam and Peter did not pay the bill, so who did?
A: Their friend, Tuesday.

Q: What fish is famous?
A: A starfish.

Q: If you were surrounded by 10 lions, 4 tigers, 3 grizzly bears and 4 leopards, how could you escape?
A: Wait until the merry-go-round stops and get off.

Q: Why did the man throw away all the new pennies he had?
A: Because they were a nuisance (new cents).

Q: Why do flies walk on the ceiling?
A: If they walked on the floor, someone might step on them.

Q: Why did the nutty kid throw butter out of the window?

A: He wanted to see a butterfly.

Q: What gets broken without being held?
A: A promise.

Q: What famous dance music did Charles Dickens write?
A: "Oliver Twist."

Q: Is it dangerous to swim on a full stomach?
A: Yes. It is better to swim in water.

Q: Why did the teacher give the zombie bad marks?
A: He was always making a ghoul (fool) of himself.

Q: Why do gardeners hate weeds?
A: Give weeds an inch and they'll take a yard.

Q: What is always coming but never arrives?
A: Tomorrow.

Q: What do you call someone who hates operas?
A: An operator (opera-hater).

Q: People's houses have rooms. What does Dracula's house have?
A: Glooms.

Q: Why did the tree need less sunshine?
A: Because it was sycamore (sick of more).

Q: Why did the farmer plant old car parts in his garden?
A: He wanted to raise a bumper crop.

Q: What goes through towns and over hills but never moves?
A: A Road.

Q: What is a boiling kettle's favourite song?
A: "Home on the Range."

Q: What did the kangaroo say when her baby was missing?
A: "Help! My pocket's been picked."

Q: Where do you put letters to boys?
A: In a mail (male) box.

Q: Why are mosquitoes annoying?
A: Because they get under your skin.

Q: What has Eighty-eight keys but can't open a single door?
A: A piano.

Q: What is as round as the moon, as black as coal, and has a hole in the middle?
A: A phonograph record.

Q: What ghost haunted the King of England in 18th century?
A: The Spirit of '76.

Q: What musical instrument from Spain helps you fish?
A: A cast-a-net (castanet).

Q: When does a female deer need money?
A: When she doesn't have a buck.

Q: What has a neck but no head?
A: A bottle.

Q: What is an opera?
A: In an opera people sing before they die.

Q: What happened when the chimney got angry?
A: It blew its stack.

Q: When are club dues paid?
A: On Duesday (Tuesday).

Q: What was the highest mountain before Mt. Everest was discovered?
A: Mt. Everest.

Q: A monkey, a squirrel, and a bird are racing to the top of a coconut tree. Who will get the banana first, the monkey, the squirrel, or the bird?
A: None of them, because you can't get a banana from a coconut tree.

Q: What is a vampire's favourite song?
A: "Fangs (thanks) for the Memory."

Q: What did the leopard say when he swallowed the man?
A: "That hit the spot!"

Q: When did the fly fly?
A: When the spider spied her.

Q: When you take away two letters from this five-letter word, you get one. What word is it?

A: Stone.

Q: Which eight-letter word still remains a word after removing each letter from it?
A: Starting-Staring-String-Sting-Sing-Sin-In-I.

Q: What is a perfect name for a selfish girl?
A: Mimi (me, me).

Q: What criminals can you find in a shoe store?
A: A pair of sneakers.

Q: When is a green book not a green book?
A: When it is read (red).

Q: What has a head but never weeps, has a bed but never sleeps, can run but never walks, and has a bank but no money?
A: A river.

Q: What is a musical pickle?
A: A piccolo.

Q: What did one clock say to the other clock when it was frightened?
A: "Don't be alarmed."

Q: When is a grown man still a child?
A: When he is a miner (minor).

Q: Where do black birds drink?
A: At a crowbar.

Q: Why did the reporter put a flashlight into his mouth?

A: He wanted to get the inside story.

Two fathers and two sons go on a fishing trip. They each catch a fish and bring it home. Why do they only bring 3 home?
A: The fishing trip consists of a grandfather, a father and a son.

Q: What is a horse's favourite song?
A: "Big Horse (because) I Love You."

Q: What did one cucumber say to the other cucumber?
A: "If you kept your big mouth shut, we wouldn't be in this pickle."

Q: When is a letter damp?
A: When it has postage due (dew).

Q: Which is more important, the sun or the moon?
A: The moon. It shines when it is dark, but the sun shines when it is light anyway.

Q: What can you hear but not touch or see?
A: Your voice.

Q: What is a ghost's favourite song?
A: "A-Haunting We Will Go."

Q: What did one skunk say to the other skunk when they were cornered?
A: "Let us spray."

Q: What musical instrument doesn't tell the truth?
A: A lyre (liar).

Q: Who settled in the West before anyone else?
A: The sun.

Q: What starts with "P" and ends with "E" and has more than 1000 letters?
A: A post office.

Q: What is a fund for needy musicians?
A: A band aid.

Q: What did the cork say to the bottle?
A: "If you don't behave yourself, I'll plug you."

Q: Where do pencils come from?
A: From Pennsylvania.

Q: Who was older, David or Goliath?
A: David must have been because he rocked Goliath to sleep.

Q: What loses its head in the morning but gets it back at night?
A: A pillow.

Q: What is a dance for two containers?
A: The can-can.

Q: What did the coward say to the stamp?
A: "I bet I can lick you."

Q: Where do you end up if you smoke too much?
A: Coffin (coughin').

Q: Why are cards like wolves?

A: Because they belong to a pack.

Q. What is something you will never see again?
A. Yesterday.

Q: What is a car fender's favourite song?
A: "Fender (when the) Moon Shines Over the Mountain."

Q: What did the delicatessen sell after it burned down?
A: Smoked meats.

Q: What do you throw out when you want to use it, but take in when you don't want to use it?
A: An anchor.

Q: Where did the rancher take the sheep?
A: To the bah-bah (barber) shop.

Q: Why are country people smarter than city people?
A: Because the population is denser in big cities.

Q: Jack rode into town on Friday and rode out 2 days later on Friday. How can that be possible?
A: Friday is his horse's name.

Q: What is avoidance?
A: A dance for people who hate each other.

Q: What do you call a worn-out rifle?
A: A shotgun (shot gun).

Q: What would happen if everyone in the country bought a pink car?

A: We would have a pink carnation (car nation).

Q: When can't astronauts land on the moon?
A: When it is full.

Q: Can you name the two days starting with T besides Tuesday and Thursday?
A: Today and tomorrow.

Q: What kind of band doesn't make music?
A: A rubber band.

Q: What is a rifle with three barrels?
A: A trifle.

Q: A man rode into town on Tuesday and stayed in a hotel. Two nights later he rode home on Tuesday. How?
A: Tuesday is the name of his horse.

Q: What kind of tie does a pig wear?
A: A pigsty (pig's tie).

Q: What is the difference between lightning and electricity?
A: We pay for electricity.

Q: What is round on both sides but high in the middle?
A: Ohio.

Q: What keeps out bugs and shows movies?
A: Screens.

Q: What is a skunk's best defence against enemies?

A: Instinct.

Q: What can run but can't walk?
A: Water.

Q: What letter stands for a drink?
A: The letter T.

Q: What is the dirtiest word in the world?
A: Pollution.

Q: If two's company and three's a crowd, what are four and five?
A: Nine.

Q: What is the favourite ride of ghost children?
A: The roller ghoster (coaster).

Q: What is a torpedo?
A: A seashell (sea shell).

Q: What kind of coat can you only put on when it's wet?
A: A coat of paint.

Q: What man in the Bible was the busiest doctor?
A: Job, because he had the most patience (patients).

Q: What is the snappiest snake?
A: A garter snake.

Q: What is the center of Gravity?
A: The letter V.

Q: What is the Eskimo's favourite song?

A: "Freeze (For he's) a Jolly Good Fellow."

Q: What happened when the man sat on a pin?
A: Nothing. It was a safety pin.

Q: What nuts can you hang pictures on?
A: Walnuts.

Q: What has four wheels and
A: A garbage truck.

Q: What kind of fish performs operations?
A: A sturgeon (surgeon).

Q: What is the last thing you take off before bed?
A: Your feet off the floor.

Q: What is the easiest way to get on TV?
A: Sit on your set.

Q: What did the paintbrush say to the floor?
A: "One more word and I'll shellac you!"

Q: What bird can lift the most?
A: A crane.

Q: What part of a car is the laziest?
A: The wheels. They are always tired.

Q: What kind of horse comes from Pennsylvania?
A: A filly (Philly).

Q: A lawyer, a plumber and a hat maker were walking down the street. Who had the biggest hat?
A: The one with the biggest head.

Q: What is the difference between a dancer and a duck?
A: One goes quick on her beautiful legs, the other goes quack on her beautiful legs.

Q: What did the picture say to the wall?
A: "I've been framed. "

Q: What two things can you never eat for breakfast?
A: Lunch and dinner.

Q: What newspaper do cows read?
A: The Daily Moos.

Q: What kind of leopard has red spots?
A: A leopard with measles.

Q: What kind of room has no doors or windows?
A: A mushroom.

Q: What is the difference between a ballerina and a duck?
A: One dances Swan Lake, the other swims in it.

Q: What diploma do criminals get?
A: The third degree.

Q: If you were in a race and passed the person in 2nd place, what place would you be in?
A: 2nd.

Q: What Roman numeral can climb a wall?
A: IV (ivy).

Q: What kind of person is fed up with people?
A: A cannibal.

Q: I have keys but no locks. I have space but no room. You can enter but can't go outside. What am I?
A: A keyboard.

Q: What is in fashion but always out of date?
A: The letter F.

Q: What did the rug say to the floor?
A: "I've got you covered."

Q: What grows up while growing down?
A: A goose.

Q: What tree is hairy?
A: A fir (fur) tree.

Q: What kind of pigeon sits down a lot?
A: A stool pigeon.

Q: What is next in this sequence: JFMAMJJASON?
A: The letter D. The sequence contains the first letter of each month.

Q: What is green and sings?
A: Elvis Parsley.

Q: What do you call a man when a Marine sits on him?
A: A submarine.

Q: If two's company and three's a crowd, what are four and five?

A: Nine.

Q: What vegetable is dangerous to have aboard ship?
A: A leek (leak).

Q: What is a ticklish subject?
A: The study of feathers.

Q: A man was cleaning the windows of a 25 story building. He slipped and fell off the ladder, but wasn't hurt. How did he do it?
A: He fell off the 2nd step.

Q: What kind of book does Frankenstein like to read?
A: A novel with a cemetery plot.

Q: What is a hangman's favourite reading material?
A: A noosepaper (newspaper).

Q: What four days of the week start with the letter "T"?
A: Tuesday, Thursday, today and tomorrow.

Q: What kind of kitten works for the Red Cross?
A: A first-aid kit.

Q: What is the difference between an oak tree and a tight shoe?
A: One makes acorns, the other makes corns ache.

Q: How many seconds are there in a year?
A: 12. (January 2nd, February 2nd, March 2nd....)

Q: What song do monsters sing at- Christmas time?
A: "Deck the halls with poison ivy, Fal-la la, la-la . . . "

Q: What is big and white and is found in Florida?
A: A lost polar bear.

Q: What can you catch but not throw?
A: A cold.

Q: What happens when two bullets get married?
A: They have a BB (baby).

Q: What insects talk too much?
A: Moths. They are always chewing the rag.

Q: One night, a butcher, a baker and a candlestick maker go to a hotel. When they get their bill, however, it's for four people. Who's the fourth person?
A: One night can also mean one knight. That makes four: one knight, a butcher, a baker and a candlestick maker.

Q: What should you do if your dog swallows a book?
A: Take the words right out of his mouth.

Q: What is in the army and is corny?
A: A colonel (kernel).

Q: How much dirt is in a hole 5 feet wide and 4 feet deep?
A: None.

Q: What did the werewolf write on his Christmas cards?
A: "Best vicious (wishes) of the season."

Q: What is a dimple?
A: A pimple going the other way.

Q: What instrument can you hear but never see?
A: Your voice. You can sing with your voice like an instrument and hear it, but no one can see it.

Q: What season is it when you are on a trampoline?
A: Springtime.

Q: What is the difference between a thief and a church bell?
A: One steals from the people, the other peals, from the steeple.

Q: How many seconds are there in a year?
A: Twelve – January 2nd, February 2nd, March 2nd…

Q: What is a forum?
A: Two-um plus two-um.

Q: What is a distant relative?
A: Someone who is not living with you.

Q: What is a word comprise of 4 letters, stills is also made of 5. Occasionally written with 12 letters and later with 5. Never written with 5 but happily with 7.
A: What, Still, Occasionally, Later, Never, Happily.

Q: What newspaper did the cavemen read?
A: The Prehistoric Times.

Q: What kind of clothes do lawyers wear?
A: Lawsuits.

Q: How many bricks does it take to complete a building made from bricks?

A: One – the last one.

Q: What is a bee?
A: An insect that stings (sings) for its supper.

Q: What is a foreign ant?
A: Important.

Q: When you do know me about me, them I am definitely something. You will always search for me. But when you know me, I am nothing. Who am I?
A: I'm a Riddle.

Q: What musical instrument does a skeleton play?
A: The trombone.

Q: What kind of Indians does Dracula like?
A: Full-blooded ones.

Q: What breaks when you say it?
A: Silence.

Q: What is a panther?
A: Someone who makes panths (pants).

Q: What is a hot and noisy duck?
A: A firequacker.

Q: I have all the knowledge you have. But I am small as your fist that your hands can hold me. Who am I?
A: I'm your brain.

Q: What large instrument do you carry in your ears?
A: Drums.

Q: What kind of puzzle makes people angry?
A: A crossword puzzle.

Q: What begins with an 'E' and ends with an 'E' but only has one letter?
A: An envelope.

Q: What is an ant dictator?
A: A tyrant.

Q: What do you always leave behind because they are dirty?
A: Your footprints.

Q: I am the biggest alphabet, as I contain the most water in the world. Who am I?
A: Alphabet 'C'.

Q: What kind of song is, "Soap, Soap, Soap, Soap, Soap?"
A: Five bars.

Q: What kind of robbery is not dangerous?
A: A safe robbery.

Q: I saw a boat full of people, yet there wasn't a single person on the boat. How?
A: They were all married.

Q: What is everyone's favourite tree?
A: A poplar (popular) tree.

Q: What is black and yellow and goes zzub, zzub?
A: A bee going backwards.

Q: I have 28 days in a month. Which month I am?
A: All months in a year have 28 days and many have more than 28 days.

Q: What kind of phone makes music?
A: A saxophone.

Q: What kind of soldier doesn't need bullets?
A: A soldier who is always shooting his mouth off.

Q: What is the best way to send a letter to the Easter Bunny?
A: By hare (air) mail.

Q: What is nothing but holes tied to holes, yet is as strong as iron?
A: A chain.

Q: Find me who am I. I am the building with number stories.
A: A Library.

Q: What kind of musician can't you trust?
A: Someone who plays the bull fiddle.

Q: What kind of spy hangs around department stores?
A: A counterspy.

Q: What is the difference between a fish and a piano?
A: You can't tuna fish.

Q: What is the best way to raise strawberries?
A: With a spoon.

Q: Scientists are trying to find out what is between earth and heaven. Can you find me?
A: AND.

Q: What kind of inning does a monster baseball game have?
A: Frightening (fright inning).

Q: What is a very hair-raising experience?
A: Visiting a rabbit farm.

Q: What holes are not holes?
A: Knotholes (not holes).

Q: What is the brightest fish?
A: Sunfish.

Q: What is the word that is spelled incorrectly in all dictionaries?
A: Incorrectly.

Q: What kind of girl does a mummy go out with?
A: Any girl he can dig up.

Q: What happens if an axe falls on your car?
A: You have an ax-i-dent (accident).

Q: What is the first thing ghosts do when they get into a car?
A: They fasten their sheet (seat) belts.

Q: What is the correct thing to do before the King of Trees?
A: Bough (bow).

Q: Everyone in the world break me when they speak every time. Who am I?
A: Silence.

Q: What kind of flower does Lassie like?
A: A cauliflower (collie flower).

Q: What Indian goes to court?
A: A Sioux (sue) Indian.

Q: What is the proverb about catching a cold?
A: "Win a flu (few), lose a flu."

Q: What is an easy way to make your money bigger?
A: Put it under a magnifying glass.

Q: A boy and an engineer were fishing. The boy is the son of the engineer but engineer is the father of the boy. Then who is the engineer?
A: Engineer is the boy's mother.

Q: What kind of dance do buns do?
A: Abundance.

Q: What is a frozen policeman?
A: A copsicle.

Q: What kind of ant can count?
A: An accountant.

Q: What is the difference between a train and a teacher?
A: A train goes "Choo-choo," but a teacher tells you to take the gum out of your mouth.

Q: Everyone in the world needs it. They generously give it. But never take it. Then what is it?
A: Advice.

Q: What would you get if you crossed a stereo and a refrigerator?
A: Very cool music.

Q: What letter should you avoid?
A: The letter A because it makes men mean.

Q: What happened when the Indian shot at Daniel Boone?
A: He had an arrow (narrow) escape.

Q: What insect is like the top of a house?
A: A tick (attic).

Q: He was driving a black truck in a long road in a great speed. The lights on the truck were off. It was a new moon day. An old lady was slowly crossing the road. He should stop the truck otherwise, he would hit the lady. How did he stop the truck?
A: The driver stopped the truck immediately after seeing the old lady, as it was bright sunny day.

Q: Who wrote, "Oh, say can you see?"
A: An eye doctor.

Q: Why did the chicken run away from home?
A: Because she was tired of being cooped up.

Q: Spell electricity with three letters.
A: NRG (energy).

Q: What do people do in China when it rains?
A: Let it rain.

Q: Four children and their pet dog were walking under a small umbrella. But none of them became wet. How?
A: It was not raining.

Q: Who was Mr. Ferris?
A: He was a big wheel in the amusement park business.

Q: Why did the cowboy get a hot seat?
A: Because he rode the range.

Q: What do you call an alligator's helper?
A: Gatorade.

Q: What brings the monster's babies?
A: Frankenstork.

Q: It is your possession and belongs to you. However, you use it very rarely. What is that?
A: Your name.

Q: Who makes up jokes about knitting?
A: A nitwit.

Q: Why did the dog run away from home?
A: Doggone if I know.

Q: What do you call a boy named Lee whom no one wants to talk to?
A: Lonely (Lone-Lee).

Q: What do you call nervous insects?

A: Jitterbugs.

Q: I'm the most slippery country in the world. Tell what am I?
A: Greece.

Q: Who has more fun when you tickle a mule?
A: He may enjoy it, but you'll get a bigger kick out of it.

Q: When do ghosts have to stop scaring people?
A: When they lose their haunting (hunting) licenses.

Q: How many times you can subtract number 3 from the number 35?
A: Only once. When you subtract number 3 from 35, it then becomes 32.

Q: What do you call your mother's other sister?
A: Deodorant (the other aunt).

Q: What do you get if you cross a kangaroo and a racoon?
A: A fur coat with pockets.

Q: You always make a more of them, but leave more of them behind you. The more you do, the more you leave behind. Tell what is it?
A: Footsteps.

Q: Where is the best place to have a bubble gum contest?
A: On a choo-choo train.

Q: What should a girl wear when she wants to end a fight?

A: Makeup.

Q: If it takes one man three days to dig a hole, how long does it take two men to dig half a hole?
A: You can't dig half a hole.

Q: What do you get if you use a natural suntan lotion?
A: A Puritan (a purer tan).

Q: What do you get if you cross a skunk and a bee?
A: An animal that stinks as it stings.

Q: Which moves faster? Heat or Cold?
A: Heat. Because many catches cold but cannot catch heat.

Q: Where do snowflakes dance?
A: At the snowball.

Q: What three letters in the alphabet frighten criminals?
A: F.B.I.

Q: Joe's father had three sons – Snap, Crackle and …?
A: Joe.

Q: What does a duck wear when he gets married?
A: A duxedo (tuxedo).

Q: What do you get if you cross a worm and a fur coat?
A: A caterpillar.

Q: There is a kind of fish that can never swim. What is that?
A: Dead fish.

Q: Where do mummies go when they visit Arizona?
A: The Petrified Forest.

Q: What was the most dangerous time for knights?
A: Nightfall (knight fall).

Q: The more you have of it, the less you see. What is it?
A: Darkness.

Q: What do you call a bee born in May?
A: A maybe.

Q: What goes snap, crackle, pop?
A: A firefly with a short circuit.

Q: Is an old 50 rupee note worth more than a new one?
A: Yes of course. 50 rupees is more valuable than 1 rupee.

Q: Where do golfers dance?
A: At the golf ball.

Q: What weapon is most feared by knights?
A: A can opener.

Q: What has one head, one foot and four legs?
A: A bed.

Q: What fruit would a gorilla like to sleep on?

A: An ape-ri-cot (apricot).

Q: What do you call cattle that sit on the grass?
A: Ground beef.

Q: What building has more and more stories than any story book?
A: A Library.

Q: When do ghosts haunt skyscrapers?
A: When they are in high spirits.

Q: When did the criminal get smart?
A: When the judge threw the book at him.

Q: What happened to the wolf who fell into the washing machine?
A: He became a wash and werewolf.

Q: What insect curses in a low voice?
A: A locust.

Q: How many apples grow on a tree?
A: All apples grow on trees only.

Q: Where do chickens dance?
A: At the fowl ball.

Q: What would happen if black widow spiders were as big as horses?
A: If one bit you, you could ride it to the hospital.

Q: What fur do you get from a skunk?
A: As fur (far) as possible.

Q: What happens to grapes that worry too much?
A: They get wrinkled and turn into raisins.

Q: A truck driver was going on by the one-way road opposing traffic. The traffic police noticed him and but took no action against him. Why?
A: He was just walking.

Q: Where do butchers dance?
A: At the meatball.

Q: What would you get if Batman and Robin were run over by a herd of stampeding elephants?
A: Flatman and Ribbon.

Q: Imagine it was raining heavily. You were in a room with no windows. The door was locked and you cannot open the door. The room was gradually filling with water and in a few minutes, the room will be drowned. How do you escape?
A: Just stop imagining.

Q: What geometric figure is like a runaway parrot?
A: A polygon (Polly gone).

Q: What has a head, a tail, four legs, and sees equally from both ends?
A: A blind mule.

Q: Which is faster among the two? Hot or cold?
A: Definitely Hot is faster, as you can easily catch cold.

Q: Where did King Arthur go for entertainment?
A: To a nightclub (knight club).

Q: What would you have if your car's motor was in flames?
A: A fire engine.

Q: If I have it, I don't share it. If I share it, I don't have it. What is it?
A: A secret.

Q: What girl's name is like a letter?
A: Kay (K).

Q: What helps keep your teeth together?
A: Toothpaste.

Q: What you can put in a heavy wooden box that can make it weigh lighter?
A: Holes.

Q: Why are comedians like doctors?
A: Because they keep people in stitches.

Q: Why couldn't the clock be kept in jail?
A: Because time was always running out.

Q: The one who made it didn't want it. The one who bought it didn't need it. The one who used it never saw it. What is it?
A: A coffin.

Q: What did the pen say to the paper?
A: "I dot an 'I' on you."

Q: What do Indians raise that you can get lost in?
A: Maize (maze).

Q: It is just something that everybody does at the same time. What is that?
A: Grow older.

Q: Why did the comedian tell jokes to the eggs?
A: He wanted to crack them up.

Q: When is a clock nervous?
A: When it is all wound up.

Q: What can be as big as an elephant but weigh nothing?
A: Its shadow.

Q: What did the bookworm say to the librarian?
A: "Can I burrow (borrow) this book?"

Q: What did the cotton plant say to the farmer?
A: "Stop picking on me!"

Q: You can hold it without seeing or touching it. What is that?
A: Your Breath.

Q: Why did the boy get a dachshund?
A: Because his favourite song was, "Get Along Little Dogie."

Q: When is an army totally destroyed?
A: When it is in quarters.

Q: What belongs to you but is used more by others?
A: Your name.

Q: Spell Indian tent with two letters.

A: TP.

Q: What did the coughing frog say to the other frog?
A: "I must have a person in my throat."

Q: It always becomes white when it becomes dirty. What is that?
A: A Black board.

Q: Why couldn't anyone play cards on the ark?
A: Because Noah sat on the deck.

Q: When do public speakers steal lumber?
A: When they take the floor.

Q: What did the boy banana say to the girl banana?
A: "You have a lot of appeal."

Q: What did the dirt say to the rain?
A: "If this keeps up, my name will be mud."

Q: Jack throws a bucket of water from his balcony. Why?
A: He wants to see waterfall.

Q: Why can't an elephant ride a bicycle?
A: Because he doesn't have a thumb to ring the bell.

Q: Where is the best place to hide a lawyer?
A: In a brief case.

Q: What goes up and down but never moves?
A: The temperature.

Q: What did the boy gopher say to the girl gopher?

A: "I gopher (go for) you."

Q: What did the mother worm say to the little worm who was late?
A: "Where in earth have you been?"

Q: Sam was very busy business man. Suddenly he threw away his expensive watch out of the window. Why?
A: Because he always felt time was flying and he just wants to see how time flies.

Q: Why couldn't anyone find the famous composer?
A: Because he was Haydn (hidin').

Q: When things go wrong, what can you always count on?
A: Your fingers.

Q: The more you take, the more you leave behind. What are they?
A: Footsteps.

Q: What did the boy firefly say to the girl firefly?
A: "I glow for you. "

Q: What did the father firefly say to his son?
A: "For a little fellow you're very bright."

Q: How many people are buried in a cemetery?
A: All people are buried.

Q: Why are pianos so noble?
A: Many are upright and the rest are grand.

Q: Which is better: "The house burned down" or "The house burned up?"
A: Neither. They are both bad.

Q: What gets bigger and bigger the more you take away from it?
A: A hole.

Q: What did the buffalo say to his son when he went away on a long trip?
A: "Bison!" ("Bye, son!")

Q: What did the grasshopper say to the cockroach?
A: "Bug, you man me!"

Q: What do you call a bear without ears?
A: BBBBBBBBB

Q: Why are movie stars cool?
A: Because they have so many fans.

Q: Who were the first gamblers?
A: Adam and Eve. They had a paradise (pair of dice).

Q: What gets wet while it's drying?
A: A towel.

Q: What did the jack say to the car?
A: "Can I give you a lift?"

Q: What bunch of animals can always be heard?
A: Cattle, because they go around in herds.

Q: How many bananas can you eat in an empty stomach?

A: ONLY ONE. Because when you eat one piece of banana, your stomach no longer remains empty.

Q: Why are jazz musicians so sweet?
A: Because they play in jam sessions.

Q: Why are farmers cruel?
A: Because they pull corn by the ears.

Q: Poor people have it. Rich people need it. If you eat it you die. What is it?
A: Nothing.

Q: What did the kid say when he opened his piggy bank and found nothing?
A: O I C U R M T.

Q: What did the porcupine say to the cactus?
A: "Are you my mother?"

Q: What is the major difference between a lighting and electricity?
A: Of course you don't need to pay for lightning.

Q: Why are good bowlers like labour unions?
A: Because they strike a lot.

Q: Why can't you keep secrets in a bank?
A: Because of all the tellers.

Q: Forward I am heavy, but backward I am not. What am I?
A: Ton.

Q: What did the paper say to the pencil?

A: "Write on!"

Q: What did the tree say to the axe?
A: "I'm stumped."

Q: It always stays hot even when put in refrigerator. What is that?
A: PEPPER.

Q: Why did the elephant paint himself all different colours?
A: So, he could hide in the crayon box.

Q: Why did the dragon swallow the pesky knight?
A: Because he was a pill.

Q: What word is spelled wrong in all the dictionaries?
A: Wrong.

Q: What did the beaver say to the tree?
A: "It's been nice gnawing (knowing) you."

Q: What children live in the ocean?
A: Life buoys (boys).

Q: It has only a head and a tail. What is that?
A: A coin.

Q: Why is a phonograph needle like a chicken?
A: They both scratch.

Q: Why is an eye like a man being flogged?
A: Because it's under the lash.

Q: If the ruler of Russia was called the Czar and his wife the Czarina, what were his children called?
A: Sardines.

Q: In what way are the letter "A" and noon the same?
A: Both are in the middle of day.

Q: It makes more noise than a dog in your house. What is that?
A: Two dogs.

Q: Why is a crossword puzzle like a quarrel?
A: Because one word leads to another.

Q: Why is it confusing when a dog growls and wags his tail at the same time?
A: It's hard to know which end to believe.

Q: What has hands but can't clap?
A: A clock.

Q: If you add 2-forget and 2-forget, what do you get?
A: 4-gotten.

Q: How can a leopard change his spots?
A: Move to another place.

Q: How can you say that an ocean is so friendly to you?
A: Because it always waves.

Q: Why doesn't the piano work?
A: Because it only knows how to play.

Q: Why is it hard to steal pigs?

A: Because pigs are squealers.

Q: If you put three ducks in a carton, what do you get?
A: A box of quackers.

Q: What advice can you give a fish so he can avoid being caught?
A: Don't fall for any old line.

Q: Lucky Sona fell off a 100 steps staircase without getting hurt. How?
A: She fell off the last step.

Q: Why do witches fly on broomsticks?
A: It beats walking.

Q: Why is a banana peel on the sidewalk like music?
A: Because if you don't C sharp you'll B flat.

Q: What is as light as a feather but even the strongest man in the world can't hold it for long?
A: His breath.

Q: A man and a dog were going down the street. The man rode, yet walked. What was the dog's name?
A: Yet.

Q: What animal talks the most?
A: A yackety-yak.

Q: X is mightier than GOD. Rich people always need X. Poor people always have X. However, if you eat X you will surely die. What is X?
A: Nothing.

Q: Why did they have to put a fence around the cemetery?
A: Because so many people were dying to get in.

Q: Why did the kid punch the bed?
A: His mother told him to hit the hay.

Q: Which letter of the alphabet has the most water?
A: The 'C'.

Q: What animal would you like to be on a cold day?
A: A little otter (hotter).

Q: What animals didn't come on the ark in pairs?
A: Worms. They came in apples.

Q: I have foot, but there are no legs. What Am I?
A: A snail.

Q: Why did the tightrope walker always carry his bank book?
A: In order to check his balance.

Q: Why did the hens refuse to lay any more eggs?
A: Because they were tired of working for chicken feed.

Q: If you took two apples from three apples how many apples would you have?
A: Two apples – the two that you took.

Q: What are two fibs?
A: A paralyse (pair of lies).

Q: What are arithmetic bugs?

A: Mosquitoes. They add to misery, subtract from pleasure, divide your attention, and multiply quickly.

Q: I always come down and never ever go up?
A: Rain.

Q: Why did the owl make everyone laugh?
A: Because he was a howl.

Q: Why did the outlaw carry a bottle of glue when he went to rob the stagecoach?
A: He wanted to stick up the passengers.

Q: What needs an answer but doesn't ask a question?
A: A telephone.

Q: What cat owes money?
A: A pussywillow (pussy will owe).

Q: During what season do ants eat most?
A: Summer. That is when they go to a lot of picnics.

Q: If I drink something, then I am just over. However, I can eat anything. What Am I?
A: A fire.

Q: Why did the football player marry the girl?
A: Because he thought she would be faithful to the end.

Q: Why does Father Time wear bandages?
A: Because day breaks and night falls.

Q: What did one tooth say to the other tooth?
A: "Thar's gold in them thar fills."

Q: What did the bald man say when he got a comb?
A: "I'll never part with it."

Q: I look taller when I am young. But as I get old, I become shorter and shorter. What Am I?
A: A candle.

Q: Why did the mother put her baby on the phonograph?
A: It had an automatic changer.

Q: Why did the robber take a bath?
A: So he could make a clean getaway.

Q: What type of cheese is made backwards?
A: Edam.

Q: What animal is a cannibal?
A: An anteater (aunt eater).

Q: What did one firefly say to the other firefly when his light went out?
A: "Give me a push. My battery is dead."

Q: I travel all over the world. But I could not move, just stay in a same single spot. What Am I?
A: A stamp.

Q: Why did the little kid dance on the jar of jam?
A: Because the top said, "Twist to open."

Q: Why did the sheriff arrest the tree?
A: Because its leaves rustled.

Q: What stays where it is when it goes off?

A: An alarm clock.

Q: What colour was the "Keep off the Grass" sign?
A: G'way (gray).

Q: What did one shrub say to the other shrub?
A: "Am I bushed!"

Q: You always carry me in your hand, always with you, from your birth till your death. I am a tree. What Am I?
A: A palm.

Q: Why did the kid put his head on the piano?
A: Because he wanted to play by ear.

Q: Why did the spy speak in a whisper?
A: Because he was on a hush-hush mission.

Q: What has one eye but can't see?
A: A needle.

Q: What did Delaware?
A: She wore her New Jersey.

Q: What did one termite say to the other termite when he saw a house burning?
A: "Barbecue tonight!"

Q: I visit you every night even if you don't call me. I'm lost every day. What Am I?
A: Stars.

Q: Why did the kid put a flashlight on his stomach?
A: He wanted to watch bellyvision (television).

Q: Why do people beat their clocks?
A: To kill time.

Q: What did Mason say to Dixon?
A: "We've got to draw the line somewhere."

Q: What did Ben Franklin say when he discovered that lightning was electricity?
A: Nothing. He was too shocked.

Q: I am always will be coming, but I will never come. What Am I?
A: Tomorrow.

Q: Why did the girl call herself an experienced actress?
A: She broke her leg and was in a cast for six months.

Q: Why does a dog chasing a rabbit resemble a bald-headed man?
A: He makes a little hare (hair) go a long way.

Q: How do you make the number one disappear?
A: Add the letter 'G' and it's Gone.

Q: What did one raindrop say to the other raindrop?
A: "My plop is bigger than your plop."

Q: What did one toad say to the other toad?
A: "One more game of leapfrog and I'll croak."

Q: I have more than 80 keys, but I cannot open any lock. What Am I?
A: A piano.

Q: Why is a violin like an auto?
A: It is best when tuned up.

Q: Why is a thief like a thermometer on a hot day?
A: Because they are both up to something.

Q: How many months of the year have 28 days?
A: All of them.

Q: How much is 5Q and 5Q?
A: 10Q.
A2: "You're welcome. "

Q: If you throw a pumpkin in the air, what comes down?
A: Squash.

Q: I will lose my head in the mornings, but I will always gain it at night. What Am I?
A: A pillow.

Q: Why was William Shakespeare able to write so well?
A: Because where there's a Will, there's a way.

Q: Why is the ocean angry?
A: Because it has been crossed so many times.

Q: A man had two sons and named them both Ed. How come?
A: Two Eds (heads) are better than one.

Q: If a rooster laid a brown egg and a white egg, what kind of chicks would hatch?

A: None. Roosters don't lay eggs.

Q: It was a green house. Inside the green house there was a white house. Inside the white house there was a red house. Inside the red house there were lots of babies. What is it?
A: A watermelon.

Q: Why was the phonograph record nervous?
A: You would be too if you lived on spins and needles.

Q: Why is your heart like a policeman?
A: Because it follows a regular beat.

Q: What has a neck but no head?
A: A bottle.

Q: How do mountains hear?
A: With mountaineers.

Q: How can you eat an egg without breaking its shell?
A: Ask someone else to break it.

Q: My best buddy always makes mistakes. But I would easily get rid of the mistakes. What Am I?
A: An eraser.

Q: Why was night baseball started?
A: Because bats like to sleep in the daytime.

Q: Why is law like the ocean?
A: Because most trouble is caused by the breakers.

Q: How do you spell "we" with two letters without using the letters W and E?

A: U and I.

Q: If an electric train travels 90 miles an hour in a westerly direction and the wind is blowing from the north, in which direction is the smoke blowing?
A: There is no smoke from an electric train!

Q: When you have me more, you can see only less. What Am I?
A: Darkness.

Q: Why is the circusman who was shot out of the cannon not working anymore?
A: Because he was discharged.

Q: Why is a sinking ship like a person in jail?
A: Because it needs bailing out.

Q: How many ghosts are there in the nation?
A: There must be a lot ghost-to-ghost (coast-to-coast).

Q: If there were ten cats in a boat and one jumped out, how many would be left?
A: None, because they were all copycats.

Q: I am a vehicle. I spell the same when you read me forwards as well as backwards. What Am I?
A: RACE CAR (try it)

Q: Why is Lassie like a comet?
A: They both are stars with tails.

Q: Why is a dictionary dangerous?
A: Because it has "dynamite" in it.

Q: How many peas are there in a pint?
A: There is only one P in "pint."

Q: If we breathe oxygen in the daytime, what do we breathe at night?
A: Nitrogen.

Q: I weigh almost nothing. I am lighter than air. But even the strongest man in the world cannot lift me. What Am I?
A: Bubble.

Q: Why should a clock never be put upstairs?
A: It might run down and strike one.

Q: How can you spell rot with two letters?
A: DK (decay).

Q: If a farmer raises wheat in dry weather, what does he raise in wet weather?
A: An umbrella.

Q: Why should you leave your watch home when you take an aeroplane?
A: Because time flies anyway.

Q: I am a five-letter word and very strong. I become single when you remove two letters from me. What Am I?
A: Stone.

Q: Why were the tennis players arrested?
A: Because, they were involved with racquets (rackets).

Q: How can you shorten a bed?

A: Don't sleep long in it.

Q: Why do postmen carry letters?
A: Because the letters can't go anywhere by themselves.

Q: How many apples can you put in an empty box?
A: Zero. When you put an apple, it no longer remains empty.

Q: Why were screams coming from the kitchen?
A: The cook was beating the eggs.

Q: How can you tell that a cat likes the rain?
A: Because when it rains it purrs (pours).

Q: Why do people always say to you, "A penny for your thoughts?"
A: Because that's all they are worth.

Q: How do you divide 20 oranges equally to 11 girls? No one gets more and no one gets less. All 11 girls should receive equal portions. How?
A: Juice the oranges and serve the equal quantity of orange juice.

Q: Why wasn't the girl afraid of the shark?
A: Because it was a man-eating shark.

Q: Can you spell a composition with two letters?
A: SA (essay).

Q: How can you keep a rooster from crowing on Monday morning?
A: Eat him for dinner on Sunday.

Q: Why does a mother carry her baby?
A: The baby can't carry the mother.

Q: It was a pink house. It was constructed with 4 walls. All walls of the house were built facing the south direction. A bear circled around the house. Now tell me what is the color of the bear?
A: It is a white bear, because the house is on the North Pole.

Q: Why was the skunk arrested for counterfeiting?
A: Because he gave out bad scents (cents).

Q: Can you spell a pretty girl with two letters?
A: QT (cutey).

Q: How can you tell where a bear lives?
A: Look for his Denmark (den mark).

Q: Why does a pencil seem heavy when you write with it for a long time?
A: Because it is full of lead.

Q: It was very dark. There was no electricity in the house. They had no candles or lanterns. The house was completely dark. A girl was reading and preparing for her exams. How?
A: Simple. The girl was blind and she was reading through Braille method.

Q: Why was the musician arrested?
A: He got into treble (trouble).

Q: Can you spell soft and slow with two letters?
A: EZ.

Q: How can you tune into the sun?
A: Use a sundial.

Q: Why is a fish like a person who talks too much?
A: Because it doesn't know when to keep its mouth shut.

Q: Tom was a clerk at a butcher shop. His height is six feet and three inches. He wears shoes sized number 12. What does he weigh?
A: He weighs meat.

Q: Why was the lobster arrested?
A: Because he was always pinching things.

Q: Can you spell very happy with three letters?
A: XTC (ecstasy).

Q: How did the big mountain know that the little mountain was fibbing?
A: Because it was only a bluff.

Q: Why do we buy clothes?
A: Because we can't get them free.

Q: We are a family of 12 members. I am the second. I am also the youngest in our family. Who am I?
A: FEBRUARY. A year has 12 months and February is the second month.

Q: Why was the lady's hair angry?
A: Because she was always teasing it.

Q: At what time do most people go to the dentist?
A: At tooth-hurty (2:30).

Q: How do birds stop themselves in the air?
A: With air brakes.

Q: Why is a toupee like a secret?
A: Because you keep it under your hat.

Q: There were two women, standing and facing the opposite ways. The first lady was facing south and the second lady was facing north. But, they could see each other. How is that?
A: They were holding the mirror.

Q: Why was the insect kicked out of the forest?
A: Because it was a litterbug.

Q: Do moths cry?
A: Sure. Haven't you ever seen a mothball (bawl)?

Q: How can you fix a short circuit?
A: Lengthen it.

Q: Why is an engaged girl like a telephone?
A: Because they both have rings.

Q: Mr. Jason was walking along the sea shore. Suddenly it started drizzling and turned into a heavy rain. He wasn't carrying any umbrella, not even any cap. He was completely wet and all his clothes were soaked in rain. Yet not even a single strand of his hair was wet. How was that possible?
A: Mr. Jason was bald.

Q: Why shouldn't you grab a tiger by his tail?
A: It may only be his tail, but it could be your end.

Q: How can you spell chilly with two letters?
A: IC (icy).

Q: How do you know that bees are happy?
A: Because they hum while they work.

Q: Why shouldn't you tell a secret to a pig?
A: Because he is a squealer.

Q: There is a basket of 5 guavas. If you take away 3 guavas, how many guavas do you have?
A: You have 3 guavas. (if you take 3, then you will have 3).

Q: Why was the dirty kid arrested?
A: For grime (crime).

Q: How can you prove that a horse has six legs?
A: A horse has four legs (forelegs) in front and two behind.

Q: How do rabbits keep their fur neat?
A: They use a harebrush (hairbrush).

Q: Why shouldn't you put grease on your hair the night before a test?
A: If you did, everything might slip your mind.

Q: If you had 5 potatoes and had to divide them equally between 3 people, what should you do?
A: Mash them first.

Made in the USA
Columbia, SC
27 November 2022